Two Comedies

When I Snap My Fingers
Mary, Mary

Bruce Adam

A Samuel French Acting Edition

SAMUELFRENCH.COM
SAMUELFRENCH-LONDON.CO.UK

Copyright © 2014 by Bruce Adam
All Rights Reserved

Cover design by Gene Sweeney

WHEN I SNAP MY FINGERS and *MARY, MARY* are fully protected under the copyright laws of the United States of America, the British Commonwealth, including Canada, and all other countries of the Copyright Union. All rights, including professional and amateur stage productions, recitation, lecturing, public reading, motion picture, radio broadcasting, television and the rights of translation into foreign languages are strictly reserved.

ISBN 978-0-573-11029-0

www.SamuelFrench.com
www.SamuelFrench-London.co.uk

For Production Enquiries

United States and Canada
Info@SamuelFrench.com
1-866-598-8449

United Kingdom and Europe
Plays@SamuelFrench-London.co.uk
020-7255-4302

Each title is subject to availability from Samuel French, depending upon country of performance. Please be aware that *WHEN I SNAP MY FINGERS* and *MARY, MARY* may not be licensed by Samuel French in your territory. Professional and amateur producers should contact the nearest Samuel French office or licensing partner to verify availability.

CAUTION: Professional and amateur producers are hereby warned that *WHEN I SNAP MY FINGERS* and *MARY, MARY* are subject to a licensing fee. Publication of this play does not imply availability for performance. Both amateurs and professionals considering a production are strongly advised to the appropriate agent before starting rehearsals, advertising, or booking a theatre. A licensing fee must be paid whether the titles are presented for charity or gain and whether or not admission is charged. Professional/Stock licensing fees quoted upon application to Samuel French.

No one shall make any changes in these titles for the purpose of production. No part of this book may be reproduced, stored in a retrieval system, or transmitted in any form, by any means, now known or yet to be invented, including mechanical, electronic, photocopying, recording, videotaping, or otherwise, without the prior written permission of the publisher. No one shall upload these titles, or part of these titles, to any social media websites.

For all enquiries regarding motion picture, television, and other media rights, please contact Samuel French.

MUSIC USE NOTE

Licensees are solely responsible for obtaining formal written permission from copyright owners to use copyrighted music in the performance of this play and are strongly cautioned to do so. If no such permission is obtained by the licensee, then the licensee must use only original music that the licensee owns and controls. Licensees are solely responsible and liable for all music clearances and shall indemnify the copyright owners of the play(s) and their licensing agent, Samuel French, against any costs, expenses, losses and liabilities arising from the use of music by licensees. Please contact the appropriate music licensing authority in your territory for the rights to any incidental music.

IMPORTANT BILLING AND CREDIT REQUIREMENTS

If you have obtained performance rights to this title, please refer to your licensing agreement for important billing and credit requirements.

CONTENTS

WHEN I SNAP MY FINGERS p.5
MARY, MARY p.37

When I Snap My Fingers

WHEN I SNAP MY FINGERS was first produced by Dunfermline Dramatic Society at Carnegie Hall Theatre on 18th April 2003. The performance was directed by Bruce Adam and Tomm Campbell, with sets by the company and lighting by Les Parker. The cast was as follows:

SVEN GALI ....Tomm Campbell
SIMON MOFFAT .... Bruce Adam
MARIA MOFFAT............................Pamela Henderson
SALLY MOFFAT .... Claire Slaughter
DAN CUTTER.................................Stephen Manson
DOLLY CUTTER ....Leonie Bisset

CHARACTERS

SVEN GALI, stage hypnotist
SIMON MOFFAT, an accountant
MARIA MOFFAT, his wife
SALLY MOFFAT, their teenage daughter
DAN CUTTER, managing director
DOLLY CUTTER, his wife

WHEN I SNAP MY FINGERS

Scene 1

(The curtain rises on the set of **SVEN** *Gali's show – "An Evening with the Master of Hypnosis". We are clearly part of the way through his performance.* **SVEN** *is putting two members of the public, whom he has hypnotised, through their paces – one of them is going round the stage on all fours behaving like a dog and the other is strutting around like a chicken.* **SIMON** *and* **MARIA** *are seated on two of the four chairs that are set out on stage apparently asleep.)*

SVEN. Here boy, here boy. Good doggie.
(The man who is behaving like a dog comes over to **SVEN** *and begins to leap up at him, trying to lick his face.)*
No – down boy; down boy. Heel. Now sit. Give me a paw. Now roll over. Roll over and play dead.
(The man is on the floor with legs and arms in the air when **SVEN** *suddenly clicks his finger.)*
And awake!
(The man looks bemused.)
What are you doing down there, sir? Let me help you up. Come and sit down here. And sleep! *(He passes his hand over the man's eyes and he appears to sleep.)* And what is this young woman doing? Tell the audience what your name is my dear.

WOMAN. Pwauk, Pwauk. Pwaauuuk!

SVEN. What a pretty name. And sleep! Before she lays an egg, ladies and gentlemen, ha, ha, ha. *(When he has deposited the woman on the other vacant chair, he turns his* *attention to* **SIMON** *and* **MARIA**.*)* And wide awake. *(He snaps his fingers.)* Good evening. And you are?

SIMON. Simon Moffat.

SVEN. And this must be your lovely wife.

MARIA. Yes, Maria

SIMON. Do you think we could just go back to our seats now? I mean, thank you for unlocking our hands and everything but...

SVEN. Tell me, Maria, do you believe in the power of hypnosis?

MARIA. Oh yes. After you told us to all clasp our hands together and then told us we were stuck fast, I couldn't unclasp my hands at all.

SVEN. And what about you Simon?

SIMON. Well, I must confess, I was a bit sceptical. I always thought that there must be some trick involved.

SVEN. What do you do, Simon?

SIMON. At the moment I'm an accountant.

SVEN. You don't look like one. Ha, ha, ha. *(He does.)* What do you mean, at the moment?

SIMON. My firm is about to be taken over by a big American company so they're reviewing our position at the present. There may be some downsizing and...

SVEN. Yes, thank you, Simon. Please leave putting the audience to sleep to me, ha, ha, ha. Do you think I could hypnotise you, Simon?

SIMON. I think I'm probably too depressed just now.

MARIA. Yes, we thought a night out – a little dinner and cabaret – might cheer us up but you were all that was on. Oh, I didn't mean...

SVEN. And sleep! Ladies and gentlemen, Sven Gali will now demonstrate the power of post-hypnotic suggestion. Maria, you wanted to be cheered up but as soon as you hear the word "Party" you will find everything very sad. Simon, when you hear the word "Funeral" you will find everything absolutely hilarious. *(He snaps his fingers.)* So, Simon, you seem a bit down about the job.

SIMON. Well, I suspect I might be made redundant.

SVEN. Gosh, funeral!

SIMON. *(laughing uproariously)* And I've been twenty years with the firm, ha, ha, ha. Twenty years down the drain, ha, ha, ha. I feel like killing myself. Ha. Ha, ha.

SVEN. Never mind. Maria's here to cheer you up. Why don't you tell us a joke, Maria? That always makes the party go with a swing.

MARIA. *(weeping copiously)* Well I'm not very good at telling jokes but, oh dear, I'm sorry. A man goes into a chemist's and asks if they have anything for wind and the ch-ch-chemist gives him a kite. Boo, hoo, hoo.

*(***SVEN*** snaps his fingers and they recover.)*

SVEN. Simon your wife's upset and you're laughing. How cruel.

SIMON. Well, I…that is…er…

SVEN. Don't stand there stammering, man, get your wife a drink.

MARIA. Oh, I never touch alcohol.

SVEN. Have a glass of water. *(He hands her a glass of water.)*

SVEN. And sleep! Simon to help your communication problem, when you hear the word "Music" you will be able to communicate only using popular songs. Maria, when you hear the word "alcohol" whatever you are drinking will become the most intoxicating thing you have ever tasted and it will render you completely drunk. *(He snaps his fingers.)* So, Simon, tell us a bit more about your work. Don't you find it stimulating?

SIMON. Well, accountancy can be quite exciting but the way things are at present…

SVEN. Music.

*(***SIMON*** sings the first verse of "Satisfaction" by The Rolling Stones.)*

SVEN. Don't you like being an accountant?

(SIMON *sings "It's a steady job," etc. from "Paperback Writer" by The Beatles.*)

MARIA. Simon, what are you doing? Make him stop, Mr Gali. Simon, what's the matter? I... *(She begins to cough, so she takes a sip of the water.)*

SVEN. I do hope you both haven't had too much alcohol.

(MARIA *suddenly begins to behave extremely drunkenly.*)

MARIA. Listen, moosh! I told you I never drink so watch it. I am stole cone slober. My God what's in this water? I feel quite sqiffy.

(SIMON *sings "How do you solve a problem like* MARIA*" from The Sound of Music.*)

MARIA. Shimon, Simon, stop being an arsh.

(SVEN *snaps his fingers and they look confused.*)

SVEN. Why, Maria, what's gotten into you?

MARIA. I... I...

SVEN. And, Simon, we never realised that beneath that humble accountant's exterior there beat the heart of a cabaret singer.

SIMON. But I never...

SVEN. Don't look so worried – you both need to relax.

SIMON. How can we relax when we're making such a spectacle of ourselves?

SVEN. And sleep! A spectacle of yourselves, eh? They haven't seen anything yet, ladies and gentlemen, Simon, give me your spectacles. Now, Simon, whenever you hear the word "glasses" your spectacles will become magic spectacles which will enable you to see everyone naked. And, speaking of naked, Maria, when you hear the word "pants" you will become a sexy striptease artiste. *(He snaps his fingers.)* Maria, you seem a bit uptight.

MARIA. Well, I am rather embarrassed.

SVEN. Don't be. I mean it's not as if we're asking you to dance round the stage dressed in a glittery top.

MARIA. I should hope not.

SVEN. And a pair of hot pants.

MARIA. I should... *(She begins to go into a sensual "bump and grind" routine.)*

SIMON. Maria, what on earth? What is she... I can't see properly – I seem to have mislaid my...

SVEN. Looking for these? *(He holds out **SIMON**'s glasses.)* Why don't you put them on?

SIMON. Thank you.

SVEN. Go ahead. Put on your glasses.

*(**SIMON** puts on the glasses. He is facing the audience and immediately reacts with shock as he examines the "naked" people. Turning to his wife – she has probably got as far as removing her jacket – he pulls off his own jacket and attempts to cover her with it. To stop the melée, **SVEN** snaps his fingers.)*

And sleep.

*(There is a disturbance in the audience, as **SALLY** jumps up.)*

SALLY. Mum, Dad, please sit down! You're making total prats of yourselves!

SVEN. Please, young lady, it is extremely dangerous to interfere when subjects are in a hypnotic state.

SALLY. They're not subjects – they're my parents and they're embarrassing enough in real life without this.

SVEN. They are in the hands of the great Sven Gali – please be seated.

*(**SALLY** reluctantly resumes her seat.)*

Ah, happy families, ladies and gentlemen. Maria, you seem to me to be a loving wife and mother.

MARIA. Yes.

SVEN. And as a loving wife, you'd never be tempted to stray.

MARIA. It's not worth it.

SVEN. Maria, when you hear the word "Romeo" you will fall madly in love with the first person you look at. Simon, are you a good father?

SIMON. Well, I think my daughter finds me a bit embarrassing at times.

SALLY. That's the understatement of the year.

SVEN. Please, young lady! I always think that parents often forget what is was like to be children themselves. So, Simon, when you hear the word "Baby" you will be four years old again. *(He snaps his fingers.)* Maria, I believe your daughter is in the audience, tonight.

MARIA. Yes, that's her over there.

SVEN. Does she know about your passion for someone other than her father?

MARIA. What?

SVEN. That there is another in your life?

MARIA. I don't know what you're...

SVEN. Maria, look at me – you know, I'm a bit of a Romeo, myself. *(**MARIA** gazes adoringly at **SVEN**.)* I mean it's not as if I'm the most attractive man in the world.

MARIA. Yes, you are.

SVEN. What was that, Maria?

MARIA. You're beautiful.

SVEN. Thank you, Maria, I think that deserves a hug.

MARIA. Yes, please. *(She grabs **SVEN** in a passionate embrace.)*

SVEN. Maria, please, not in front of the audience.

MARIA. Let's go to your dressing room.

SVEN. What about your husband?

MARIA. He's not coming. I want to be alone with you.

SIMON. Maria, what are you doing?

MARIA. Oh, Simon, don't be a killjoy – I only want to go somewhere quiet and make mad, passionate love to this gorgeous man.

SIMON. Oh, right. What?

SVEN. Yes, Simon, don't be such a baby.

SIMON. I'm not a baby. I'm not, I'm not.

SVEN. All right, you're a big boy – a big grown up accountant. Maria, please watch where you're putting your hands.

SIMON. Don't want to be count ant.

SVEN. What do you want to be?

SIMON. Train driver or or or lollipop man or or or an astr— aster— astr— a space man. Want to be a space man. Blast off! Brrrm, brrrm, whoosh! *(He runs around the stage pretending to be flying through space.)*

*(**SVEN** continues to fend off **MARIA**'s advances. **SVEN** snaps his fingers.)*

SVEN. And sleep. *(As they do so a fire alarm sounds, NB: the audience should be alerted prior to the play that there will an alarm effect and they should also be informed about the difference between the sound effect and the real alarm.)* Please, don't panic, ladies and gentlemen, just leave the building in an orderly manner. *(He goes around snapping his fingers.)* And wide awake, everyone, we have to go! *(**SVEN** exits hurriedly. The four people onstage look dazed for a moment till **SALLY** comes up and ushers them off.)*

SALLY. Come on, Mum, Dad, there's a fire. Don't want to leave you here, tempting as it may be. Come on, Miss, Mister. Don't just stand there.

(Exeunt dazedly as the curtains falls.)

Scene 2

(When the curtain rises again we are in the **MOFFAT**s' *sitting room. Sofa, armchairs, coffee table centre, a drinks table upstage right, telephone table upstage left. There are doors upstage right to the kitchen and upstage left to the hall and the rest of the house.* **SALLY** *is lounging on the sofa reading a magazine in her "uniform" of jeans and tee shirt with her ipod on.* **MARIA** *enters from upstage left still in the middle of dressing.)*

MARIA. Sally, they'll be here any minute. Get ready.

SALLY. What?

MARIA. Get ready.

SALLY. What?

*(***MARIA** *lifts one earphone away from* **SALLY***'s ear.)*

MARIA. Your father's new boss and his wife will be here soon. Get ready.

SALLY. I am ready.

MARIA. Please, Sally, you know how important this is to your father. The impression we make tonight on this new managing director and his wife may decide his future with the company.

SALLY. Mum, don't be wet. They've already decided to dump dad.

MARIA. They have not decided to dump him. Zip me up.

SALLY. Sorry. They've decided that he's superfluous to the long-tem global dynamic. Can't reach.

MARIA. Get off your bottom and do it.

*(***SALLY** *rises and zips up her mother's dress.)*

SALLY. Look, I'll just go to my room and listen to some music. Tonight's going to be completely pants.

(As **SALLY** *heads for the door,* **MARIA**, *having heard the key word, begins to strip.* **SALLY** *clicks her fingers and comes back to retrieve her book from the coffee table. And* **MARIA** *stops.)*

MARIA. Make an effort for your father's sake. Zip me up.

SALLY. I just...did. (*With a puzzled shrug, she zips her mother's dress again.*)

MARIA. Sally, you can't meet Mr Cutter and his wife dressed like that.

SALLY. Cutter, eh? How appropriate. I bet he's a typical American – really up himself.

MARIA. Please don't do anything to embarrass us tonight.

SALLY. That's rich after that little performance from you and Dad last night. I don't know what was worse – Dad the singing child or you the boozed-up slut.

MARIA. Sally! You know your father and I don't remember anything about last night.

SALLY. You were all over the greasy hypnotist.

MARIA. Will you stop going on about last night.

SALLY. I thought at one point I'd have to watch my mother dancing around in front of all those people dressed in her bra and pants. (*As she slouches back on the sofa, she fails to notice her mother beginning to strip again.*) Or Sven would take you back to his dressing room with a snap of his fingers. (*She snaps her fingers and* **MARIA** *stops.*)

MARIA. I... Go and put on a dress. And zip me up,

SALLY. What? I think you should go and change into a dress with a zip that works. (*As she zips her mother's dress again.*) Anyway I don't have a dress.

MARIA. Go and take off those jeans at once, young lady.

SALLY. Fine, I'll just meet Mr and Mrs Cutter in my pants. (*As she exits,* **MARIA** *begins to strip again.* **SIMON**'*s voice is heard from the hall.*)

SIMON. Maria, Maria, where are you? (*He enters.*) What are you doing? You're not even dressed yet. (*He snaps his fingers.*) Damn, I meant to go by the off-licence and get Cutter's favourite cognac.

(**MARIA** *begins to put her dress back on with a puzzled expression.*)

Is dinner organised? They'll be here any minute.

MARIA. It's under control. We'll have some drinks and canapés in here and then we'll go through to dinner. I must say this company that's taking over your lot must be cheapskates – why doesn't this new boss take us out to dinner?

SIMON. It's the new management way – observe the senior staff in their own environment to see if they fit into the "company family" ethos. Just before you sack them and bring in your own team.

MARIA. Come on, love. Maybe the impression we make tonight will persuade them that you're indispensable.

SIMON. Speaking of making impressions, is our daughter prepared to co-operate? Changed her mind about divorcing us after last night?

MARIA. She was embarrassed. I'm just glad I can't remember it if we did half the things she says.

SIMON. I still feel a bit funny. I hope she's not going to behave like the spawn of the devil this evening. Cutter wants his managers to be "the epicentres of their controlled internal universes".

MARIA. Ooh, we bow before you mighty Ming the Merciless.

SIMON. Very funny. If you and Sally don't help tonight, Cutter will realise I have as much control of my environment as an incontinent goldfish.

(SALLY *enters.*)

Good evening, Satan's daughter.

SALLY. Hi, Dad.

MARIA. Zip me up, dear.

(SALLY *looks puzzled as he does so.*)

SIMON. Sally, you do realise how important tonight might be?

SALLY. Chill, Dad, It's only a dinner party.

(*Having heard the trigger word,* MARIA *begins to weep.*)

MARIA. Oh God, what if they hate the meal? It's beef Wellington.

SIMON. Darling, it's all right. Don't cry.

MARIA. But what if they're vegetarians? Boo, hoo, hoo.

SIMON. Come on, love, they're Americans – they'd eat you if you were in a bun with fries.

SALLY. Mum, it's dinner for God's sake – stop being such a baby.

(**SIMON**, *having heard the trigger word, becomes a four-year-old.*)

SIMON. I don't cry. I'm tough – tougher than you. Tougher than Batman. POW, POW. (*He leaps around the room fighting imaginary opponents and scaling tall buildings.*)

MARIA. Oh dear, oh dear and now your father's gone bonkers.

SALLY. Mum, Dad, why are you behaving like this? Wait a minute! The post-hypnotic stuff! (*She snaps her fingers.*) Sven Gali!

(**SIMON** and **MARIA** *stop, looking confused.*)

SIMON. What's going on?

SALLY. Mr Creepy, that's what's going on.

MARIA. Who?

SALLY. Sven Gali, you're both still under his influence.

SIMON. Don't be silly.

SALLY. Remember how you behaved when you heard certain words?

SIMON & MARIA. (*together*) No.

SALLY. Whatever. The point is, when you hear words, you're still doing the things he programmed you to do.

MARIA. What?

SALLY. Why else are you crying for no apparent reason and Dad's behaving like Jimmy Krankie's little brother?

SIMON. I don't believe it.

SALLY. You will when one of the Cutters says the wrong word tonight and Mum starts getting her kit off.

MARIA. Surely that's all worn off by now.

SALLY. What were the words again? "Funeral" was one.

SIMON. *(laughing helplessly)* What a disaster! I'll just kiss my job goodbye as Mum serves up the starters in her birthday suit.

(**SALLY** *snaps her fingers and he stops.*)

SALLY. And "party" was another.

MARIA. *(crying once more)* Oh no, how humiliating.

(**SALLY** *snaps her fingers and she stops.*)

SALLY. And "baby".

SIMON. Hee, hee, hee. You'll be bare and everyone will be able to see your bottom.
Bum, bum, bum.

(**SALLY** *snaps her fingers and he stops. They pause as they regard one another.*)

SIMON. Oh my God!

MARIA. What are we going to do?

SALLY. I suggest we get in touch with that hypnotist.

MARIA. How?

SALLY. I'll look up the club's number in the Yellow Pages. Perhaps we can get him before he goes on stage tonight. *(She goes to the directory on the telephone table, looks up the number and begins to dial it.)*

SIMON. There's no time. They'll be here soon.

MARIA. We'll just have to avoid those words.

SIMON. We don't even know what they are.

SALLY. I'll keep an eye on you – for a small fee. *(on the telephone)* Hello, could I speak to Mr Sven Gali, please? That's as may be, but this is urgent. Look, tell him to get to the phone or there's a story going to the tabloids that will send his career down the tubes.

MARIA. Sally!

SIMON. Was that the door? *(He goes to look out of door upstage left.)*

SALLY. *(on the telephone)* Hello. Sorry, I can't hear you for the music.

(SIMON *sings "I see a little silhouetto," etc. from "Bohemian Rhapsody" by Queen.*)

MARIA. Simon!

(*There is a knock at the door.* SIMON *sings Dave Edmund's version of "I hear you knocking."*)

Simon, what are you doing?

(SIMON *sings, "I'm singin' in the rain" from the film/musical, substituting the word "room" for "rain."*)

SALLY. (*on the phone*) Hold on a minute. (*She snaps her fingers.*) Is that Mr Gali? You hypnotised my parents last night and they're still hypnotised. You have to come here and do something about it.

MARIA. Answer the door – it's them.

SIMON. How can I let them in here? We don't know what we're going to do next. Sally, you go and tell them we've been struck down with something infectious.

SALLY. (*on the phone*) One moment. (*to* SIMON) Don't be wet – let them in. I'm trying to sort this thing out now.

(SIMON *exits to answer the door.*)

(*on the phone*) Did you hear what I said? My mother's whipping her clothes off at every opportunity and crying her eyes out and my father thinks he's Gene Kelly and Freddy Mercury when he isn't being Batman and laughing like a maniac.

(MARIA *nervously pours herself a glass of water.*)

What? No, I haven't been drinking. Look, I have not had a drop of alcohol.

(MARIA, *who has been drinking her water, suddenly starts swaying drunkenly.*)

(SIMON *enters with* DANIEL *and* DOLLY CUTTER. DANIEL *is a brash, no-nonsense American and* DOLLY *is his trophy wife, clearly chosen because of her sex appeal rather than her intellectual prowess.*)

SIMON. Mr and Mrs Cutter, I'd like you to meet my wife, Maria.

MARIA. A great pleasure for you to meet me.
DANIEL. Er…yeah. Please, call me Daniel.
MARIA. Dan, Dan the funny wee man. *(She giggles.)*
DANIEL. Daniel, please, I hate Dan.
SALLY. *(on the phone)* Look, can you speak up, I can't hear you.
SIMON. How was the journey down?
DANIEL. Long.
MARIA. Would you like to use the toilet? You must be desperate, Dan. *(She giggles.)*
DANIEL. No thanks. And it's Daniel.
SIMON. On the phone is my daughter, Sally. Can I take your coat, Mrs Cutter?
DOLLY. No way, honey, Daniel just bought it for me. Oh, I get it. Sometimes I take you British guys up the wrong way.

(MARIA giggles.)

Call me Dolly.

SALLY. *(on the phone)* Will you get them to turn down the music?

(SIMON sings the first lines of "Hello Dolly" from the musical of the same name.)

Listen, I'm just going to take this in the other room. *(She snaps her fingers and exits.)*

DANIEL. Your daughter's a real charmer.
SIMON. Please sit down. Can I get you a drink?
DANIEL. Obviously you guys have already been on the sauce.
SIMON. I did have a little on my chips at lunchtime.
DANIEL. The sauce, the juice, the booze.
MARIA. I don't drink.
DANIEL. Oh, come on.

SIMON. No. It's not…it's a medical condition – sort of migraines that affect part of the brain so she sometimes seems drunk.

DOLLY. I had to go to the doctor with my brain once.

SIMON. What'll you have?

DANIEL. Scotch – straight up.

SIMON. Of course, otherwise you'd spill it. Dolly?

DOLLY. You got any tequila?

MARIA. I think there might be some left over from when Sally had her friends round the other night. I'll just get the canapés. *(She exits to the kitchen.)*

*(***SIMON*** gets the drinks.)*

DANIEL. I'm going to get straight to the point, Muffin.

SIMON. That's Moffat, sir.

DANIEL. You might think it's a little unusual – us coming round like this.

SIMON. Not at all, sir.

DANIEL. As far as we in the company are concerned, we don't just employ a guy who comes into the office for a few hours every day. When you're with us, you're with us twenty-four seven. You eat, drink, and sleep the company. Hell, you even shit the company.

*(***SIMON*** hands round the drinks.)*

SIMON. That won't do my haemorrhoids much good. Ha, ha.

DANIEL. We don't like employees who aren't serious-minded, Muffin.

SIMON. No, of course.

DANIEL. Straight down the line family men. No odd behaviour. No crap.

DOLLY. And we ladies don't like fellas who cuss, Mr.

DANIEL. Sorry, baby.

*(***SIMON*** is sipping his drink as he hears the trigger word. He spits out his drink.)*

SIMON. Uugggh, uuuggh, uuugggh. *(He rushes over to the water and swigs it straight from the jug.)* Hot, hot, hot.

(MARIA enters with a tray of canapés.)

MARIA. Here we are – please help yourselves – you must try the mushroom and quail eggs or the anchovies and roasted peppers.

(SIMON leaps over the sofa, grabs a handful and shoves them in his mouth.)

Simon!

(SIMON takes a mouthful and then tries to scrape it off his tongue.)

SIMON. Uuugggh, uuugggh, uuugggh. Horrid, horrid, horrid.

DANIEL. Are you OK, Muffin?

(SIMON starts to wriggle round clutching his groin.)

SIMON. Have to go for a wee wee. *(He dashes off.)*

MARIA. Simon! You'll have to excuse Simon; he's been under a lot of stress lately, what with the takeover and everything.

DANIEL. I hope he's not cracking up – this is a tough business and there's no room in it for guys who can't cut it.

MARIA. No, it's not that…

(SIMON rushes back in.)

SIMON. Zip, zip, can't get zip undone. Burstin' burstin'.

(MARIA undoes his zip and he rushes off again.)

MARIA. Em…he always has trouble with those trousers. *(pause)* Another drink! *(She collects their glasses and goes to the drinks table for refills.)* What do you do Dolly?

DOLLY. Shop, mostly.

MARIA. Oh that must be interesting.

DANIEL. Yeah, she spends hours in a clothes store and comes out with a belt – I go in for five minutes and come out with six shirts, two coats and three pairs of pants.

(**MARIA** *begins to strip.* **SALLY** *enters.*)

SALLY. Mum! *(She snaps her fingers and* **MARIA** *stops.)*

MARIA. Phew! It's hot in here. Don't you find it hot in here?

DOLLY. Maybe a little.

SALLY. Mum, that friend of ours – he's speaking to the club manager and phoning me back.

MARIA. *(shouting)* Phoning you back! Didn't you tell him it's a matter of life and death? *(realising the others are watching)* Em… We were in a club last night and I left my gloves.

DANIEL. What was in them – your hands?

DOLLY. I know how you feel – I left my new coat at a party the other night.

MARIA. *(weeping)* Sally, you haven't changed for dinner.

DANIEL. Hey, hey, don't worry. Jeans are fine. Some young girls these days dress like hookers.

MARIA. *(crying harder)* She does that too. She's always slopping round the house in shorts and a rugby shirt.

DANIEL. Huh?

SALLY. Mum, snap out of it. *(She snaps her fingers.)*

MARIA. Sorry. I get quite emotional about clothes.

DANIEL. We noticed.

SALLY. Where's Dad?

MARIA. Yes. Sally, why don't you go and see if he's in a trance somewhere?

SALLY. Got you.

(**SIMON** *enters, cleaning his glasses.*)

Too late.

SIMON. Dropped my specs down the toilet.

DANIEL. Pass us the drinks, Muffin.

MARIA. Sorry, I forgot.

DOLLY. Park your fanny. I'll get them.

SIMON. Ooh, she said fanny. Tee, hee, hee.

(**SALLY** *goes to her father and snaps her fingers.*)

DANIEL. You and your wife feeling OK, Muffin?

SIMON. Yes, fine.

DOLLY. I ain't sure which of these glasses is which. *(SIMON is just donning his glasses as he hears the word.)*

SIMON. I'm absolutely aahhh!

DOLLY. What's up, Simon.

SIMON. You're, you're, you're...

DOLLY. Hey, Maria, I think your husband's staring at my boobies.

SIMON. They're, they're, they're...naked.

(SALLY snaps her fingers.)

DOLLY. You British are so prudish – my dress may be a little low-cut but what the heck! If you've got it, flaunt it.

DANIEL. Besides I paid a New York surgeon a fortune for those babies.

(SIMON, reverting to his child-like persona, prods DOLLY's chest.)

SIMON. Honk, honk.

(SALLY snaps her fingers.)

DANIEL. What do you think you're doing?

SIMON. I... I've always been fascinated by plastic surgery – I was just...testing their texture.

DOLLY. *(laughing)* I hope you don't go around doing that – you could get yourself arrested, baby.

(SIMON becomes a child again and once more prods DOLLY's chest.)

SIMON. Honk, honk.

(SALLY and MARIA snap their fingers simultaneously.)

DANIEL. Will you stop that! What's going on here? Did any of you people hear what I said about odd behaviour?

DOLLY. Cool it, honey, remember your ulcer.

DANIEL. She gets all emotional about gloves and he's behaving like a kid with a breast fixation. And what's with all the fingers snapping?

MARIA. Sally and I are just practising for our Flamenco classes – weren't we darling?

SALLY. *O* bloody *lé.* I'm going to call that club again. *(She exits.)*

SIMON. Wait, what if you mother and I go off again? Ha, ha, ha. Well, what were we all talking about? Daniel, Dolly, got any more tits – I mean tips – about the kind of man you're looking for?

DANIEL. As I was trying to say, we like regular conventional guys. Last place the company took over was full of arty types and fags.

SIMON. I gave up – haven't had a fag in over a year now.

*(**DOLLY** and **DANIEL** look startled.)*

DOLLY. You haven't?

DANIEL. Well, I heard you Brits were broad-minded. But, I need people who'll fit in – be team players.

MARIA. Simon was quite sporty – we were talking about hookers earlier – Simon used to be one.

DOLLY. You were a hooker?

SIMON. Years ago – before my knees went.

DOLLY. Gosh!

DANIEL. The thing I hate most though is a guy bursting my chops and jerking me around. You hear what I'm saying?

SIMON. I hear you – I'm just not sure I understand a word of it. Let me freshen up your drinks. More water, Maria?

MARIA. I have some here.

DANIEL. No more for Dolly. I hate women who drink too much alcohol.

*(**MARIA** has an instant reaction as she sips her water.)*

DOLLY. How long have you been doing Flamingo, Maria?

MARIA. *(giggling)* Flamingo! Flamingo! You mean Flamenco, you silly cow.

DOLLY. Cow?

SIMON. Oh that's an English term of affection. Maria, what is it?

MARIA. A flamingo is a big colourful bird that spends most of its time with its head up its arse – a bit like you, Dolly.

DOLLY. Huh?

MARIA. Flamenco is a Spanish dance and I'm an exsh… exsh…good. *(She demonstrates drunkenly.)*

(SIMON joins in briefly, snapping his fingers to bring her around.)

SIMON. *Olé!*

DANIEL. Don't you think your wife's had enough?

MARIA. It's only water.

DOLLY. I love Spanish guitar music.

MARIA. Have you been to Spain?

DANIEL. I have to fly out there tomorrow to conclude some business.

(SIMON sings the first verse of "Daniel" by Elton John.)

DANIEL. You seem to be taking things pretty lightly.

DOLLY. Come on, honey, you sing in the shower.

MARIA. Simon!

(SIMON sings the first verse of "Maria" from "West Side Story." MARIA snaps her fingers.)

SIMON. What…

MARIA. You were singing, dear.

SIMON. Ha, ha. Well, I'm just so happy about Mr Cutter's philosophy about how to run an organisation. I feel like singing.

DANIEL. I'm not sure you get it, Muffin; it sure isn't going to be all singing and dancing.

SIMON. I'm aware of that, sir.

MARIA. Have you been to Britain before, Mrs Cutter?

DOLLY. Dolly, please. I came over to London a few times when Daniel had business here. Took in the sights – Harrods, Harvey Nichols, Liberty. I thought the Mall would have more shops than that cute big one that sells royal stuff.

DANIEL. Buckingham Palace.

DOLLY. Yeah, and we saw some shows – went down to Staten on Avon and took in a show by that English guy – what was his name, honey?

DANIEL. Shakespeare.

DOLLY. I think it was about these crazy teenagers who fall in love but the guy can't get at the girl 'cause she's on this balcony and he's busy running with his buddies sword fighting and stuff.

DANIEL. *Romeo and Juliet.*

(**MARIA** *has been watching* **DOLLY** *throughout this and, on hearing the trigger word, regards her with a mixture of love and desire.*)

MARIA. A story of star-crossed lovers.

DOLLY. I just didn't get it – I'm so dumb.

MARIA. Don't say that – you're intelligent and beautiful.

DOLLY. Er…thanks, honey.

MARIA. Say that again.

DOLLY. Thanks, honey?

MARIA. I love the way you call me honey.

SIMON. Can I get anyone another drink?

DANIEL. When's dinner?

SIMON. Maria? Darling?

(**MARIA** *is preoccupied, gazing at* **DOLLY**, *who is becoming rather uncomfortable.*)

DANIEL. It's just I've had a couple of glasses on kinda an empty stomach.

SIMON. Aaahhh! *(SIMON reacts to the trigger word, removing his glasses and putting them back on in amazement.)*

DOLLY. I bought this outfit in London – you don't think it's a little too revealing?

SIMON. Revealing – It's invisible! *(He puts his hand over his eyes.)*

MARIA. I love it – you have a beautiful body.

DANIEL. *(rising)* Yeah – a lot of guys think I married Dolly because of her looks. I like to think I'm a bigger guy than that.

(SIMON opens his eyes and regards him.)

SIMON. You certainly are!

DANIEL. Treat people seriously if you want to be a mover and shaker.

SIMON. Couldn't you move and shake further over there?

(MARIA has meanwhile put her arm around DOLLY and is stroking her arm as SALLY enters.)

SALLY. He's on his way. *(SIMON rushes to her, attempting to cover her with his jacket.)* What's going on?

DANIEL. Your old man's nuts.

SIMON. What about yours? Put them away.

DOLLY. I think I'd better go to the little girl's room.

MARIA. I'll come with you.

DOLLY. What?

MARIA. It's upstairs – I'll show you my bedroom on the way.

DOLLY. Well, I...

(SALLY snaps her fingers and they recover.)

SIMON. *(sotto voce)* How long did he say he'd be?

SALLY. *(sotto voce)* I told you – he's rushing here before the show.

DOLLY. Where did you say the john was?

SIMON. John who?

DOLLY. Toilet.

SIMON. John toilet?

MARIA. It's at the top of the stairs – second door on the left. I'll show you.

DOLLY. No! No, I'll find it.

MARIA. I'll just go and check dinner, then. After you.

DOLLY. You know, I don't really need to go right now after all.

MARIA. Well, don't sit there crossing your legs. I hope you like what I've got for afters, Dolly – even though I say so myself, I do very inventive things with fruit. *(She exits.)*

SALLY. I hope Mum and Dad have been keeping you entertained.

DANIEL. Entertained? Listen, I've heard about the so-called British sense of humour but I have to tell you, I don't appreciate it, Muffin.

SALLY. Isn't that nice, Dad? Mr Cutter's got a pet name for you already.

DANIEL. It's immature – you strike be as being immature.

SALLY. You've got it all wrong, Mr Cutter; my dad has no sense of humour at all.

DANIEL. I'm not saying we should go around like we're at a funeral but sometimes the laughter has to stop.

(Having heard the trigger word, **SIMON** *is furiously trying to stop himself from bursting into laughter.)*

My father, God rest his soul, died when I was real young.

SIMON. PPPPHHHH!

DANIEL. You listening to this? I had to grow up real fast to look after my mother, who was in a wheelchair.

SIMON. PPPHHH!

DANIEL. Are you feeling all right?

SIMON. HA, HA, HA, HA.

SALLY. Dad! *(She snaps her fingers.)*

SIMON. *(to* **SALLY***)* For God's sake pay attention.

SALLY. Don't be so ungrateful.

DANIEL. You're unbelievable.

SIMON. Sorry, It's just when I'm deeply moved I become a bit hysterical.

SALLY. Yes, Dad's never been able to express emotion – he doesn't know the difference between tears and laughter. Mum likes a good laugh, though. She's really fun loving.

DOLLY. Your mom – is she a little gay?

SALLY. All the time!

DOLLY. You seem very understanding.

(**MARIA** *enters.*)

SALLY. She's a real party animal.

MARIA. *(weeping)* Dinner will be another five minutes.

DOLLY. Hey, don't worry, honey – I mean, Maria. We're not starving to death here.

DANIEL. Speak for yourself.

(**SALLY** *snaps her fingers.*)

SIMON. Quicker!

SALLY. Why don't you do it yourself – I'm the one saving your skin. *(She holds out a piece of paper.)* Here, Sven gave me a list of words to avoid. Sort it out yourself till he gets here.

DANIEL. What's going on here, Muffin?

SIMON. Oh, it's words that Sally's anger management counsellor says she has to avoid.

SALLY. What?

SIMON. You know, words like never and hate and can't.

SALLY. Bugger!

SIMON. That one as well. In fact, we're expecting a brief visit from her counsellor, Sven, this evening.

SALLY. I don't believe this.

DOLLY. *(meaning well)* Oh, Sally seems like a real cow to me!

SALLY. A cow? *(mischievously looking at the list of words)* I'll tell you what makes me an angry cow shall I? Living with these two.

MARIA. Sally!

SALLY. I mean Mum has one unit of alcohol and she's drunk—

(**MARIA**'s *legs suddenly go rubbery.*)

– then she starts spoiling the party by crying.

(**MARIA** *begins to weep.*)

Meanwhile Dad doesn't care – he just laughs, says it's her funeral—

(**SIMON** *starts laughing.*)

– and goes and listens to his music.

(**SIMON** *sings Elvis Presley's "You Ain't Nothing But a Hound Dog")*

Then Mum pants after every Romeo who gives her the eye—

(**MARIA**, *still drunk and crying, begins to take off her clothes and launches herself into a spluttering and protesting* **DANIEL***'s lap, saying "Come here, you gorgeous creature."*)

– and Dad either behaves like a baby—

(**SIMON**, *still laughing, begins to point at them, singing, "Daniel and Maria up a tree, K I S S I N G."*)

– or looks at everybody through rose coloured glasses.

(**SIMON**, *shocked, points at* **DOLLY** *then throws the cover from the back of the sofa over her, laughing and singing, "I see the moon, the moon sees me".*)

(**SALLY** *snaps her fingers loudly. There is a pause as everyone freezes with shock, broken by a loud knocking at the door.*)

SALLY. I'll get it – it must be my anger management counsellor. *(She exits.)*

SIMON. I think I can explain.

DANIEL. Would you get our coats, please? We're leaving.

MARIA. But you haven't had dinner.

DANIEL. In this asylum? Are you kidding? Muffin, I'm back from Spain day after tomorrow and I want you in my office first thing. Crayon a note in your diary, Dolly, we're out of here. *(He storms out.)*

DOLLY. Well, thanks for a lovely evening, folks. *(She kisses* **SIMON** *on the cheek and is about to kiss* **MARIA** *but changes her mind and exits.)*

(After a pause, **SIMON** *goes to the door and calls off.)*

SIMON. It's MOFFAT! Well, that's that.

MARIA. Never mind, darling. That must be Mr Sven Gali at the door. He'll get us back to normal and when you see Cutter you can explain.

SIMON. Do you know, I don't really know if I want to work for "the company", anyway. *(There is a pause and then he starts to laugh.)*

MARIA. Oh my God, I must have said one of the words.

SIMON. No, no. I've just seen the funny side of all this. Did you see their faces when you offered to take Dolly up to your bedroom?

MARIA. *(joining in)* And I thought I'd die when you came in to get your trousers unzipped. *(After a moment they hug each other.)*

SIMON. What was that word?

MARIA. What word?

SIMON. The one that gives you an overwhelming urge to get your clothes off.

MARIA. Steady, little boy, you're too young – besides, my girlfriend wouldn't like it.

(They are laughing as **SALLY** *and* **SVEN** *enter.)*

SALLY. Not interrupting anything are we?

SVEN. Please accept my most sincere apologies – nothing like this has ever happened in my entire career.

SIMON. I ought to be furious with you – and you, young lady – but I suspect you may have done me a favour.

SALLY. Don't worry, I had a quick word in the bimbo's ear before she left – persuaded her to organise a home visit for her husband from my anger management counsellor.

SVEN. I think the great Sven Gali can persuade your boss that you are a wonderful asset to his organisation.

SIMON. I'm not sure about this.

SVEN. Don't worry – nothing can go wrong – you were my only mistake. Speaking of which, if you give me a moment I will remove the post-hypnotic suggestions. I must return to the club – I am on soon.

(There is a frantic knocking on the door.)

MARIA. Who could that be now?

SALLY. I'll get it. *(She exits.)*

SVEN. I must not disappoint my many fans. You know I could hardly get out of the club for them, milling around the exit. I am almost certain some of them follow me around. Ah well, the price of fame. Please, sit down and relax. Clear your minds and listen only to the sound of my voice.

*(There is a commotion and the man and woman from the first scene burst in pursued by **SALLY**. The woman is squawking and the man is growling. The woman proceeds to peck angrily at **SVEN**'s head and the man, on all fours, to bite his leg.)*

SVEN. Help! Get them off me!

(The others are attempting to do so as:)

(The curtain falls.)

Mary, Mary

MARY, MARY was first produced by Dunfermline Dramatic Society at Carnegie Hall Theatre on 5th April 2002. The performance was directed by Les Parker, with sets by Tomm Campbell and Pamela Henderson and lighting by Neil McCallum. The cast was as follows:

MARY WILSON . . . . Mary Parker
MARY MACKENZIE . . . . Leonie Bisset
TERRY WILSON . . . . Tomm Campbell
MARY LEVIN . . . . Pamela Henderson

CHARACTERS

TERRY WILSON, 30s, widower
MARY WILSON, his mother, eccentric, linguistically challenged
MARY MACKENZIE, young, sober
MARY LEVIN, young, drunk

MARY, MARY

(A living room. Sofa downstage right, small table centre, chairs upstage centre and downstage left. Door upstage centre.)

(When the curtain rises **MARY MACKENZIE** *is sitting rather awkwardly on the sofa.* **MARY WILSON** *enters from the kitchen with crisps and dip.)*

WILSON. Here we are, Mary, some crisps and dips. Just help yourself. Dinner won't be long. I hope Terry hasn't gone to the pub. He already drinks far too much in my view. Can I offer you a drink – gin?

MAC. I don't drink – something soft perhaps?

WILSON. Or perhaps we ought to wait for Terry. Have a crisp and dip.

*(***MAC*** takes a crisp and is about to dip it when:)*

WILSON. No! Not that one! That's the garlic – play your cards right and you never know, eh?

MAC. I'm not sure I…

WILSON. Breath.

MAC. What?

WILSON. Garlic breath – not good for, what is it you youngsters call it – shagging?

MAC. I beg your…

WILSON. No that's not it – snogging, that's it.

MAC. Listen, Mrs Wilson…

WILSON. Boys don't kiss girls with myxomatosis, do they?

MAC. Mrs Wilson…

WILSON. Mary, please. Isn't it a coincidence? Both of us being called Mary.

MAC. Yes, it's such an unusual name. Mrs Wilson, I'm not sure this is such a good idea.

WILSON. This is just a little dinner – no pressure. It's just I'm keen to get my Terry out and about again after... well, you heard about his wife, of course.

MAC. I had heard something about Terry being a widower. I've only just joined the staff so...

WILSON. Tragic really. Thirty-four.

MAC. Had she been ill?

WILSON. Run down.

MAC. After a long illness?

WILSON. By a furniture van.

MAC. Oh.

WILSON. Reversed right over her, they say.

MAC. How dreadful.

WILSON. I can't understand how she didn't hear it. They usually make noises when they reverse don't they? Beep, beep, beep. Mind you, Avril never did concentrate. I've seen me speaking to her for hours and she just sat there with a glazier expression on her face. Terry nearly saw it you know – he was in the high street just after it. They were just cleaning up the blood – have some of that red dip, it's so lovely.

MAC. Mrs Wilson...

WILSON. Mary, dear, please. Yes, I was speaking to Avril only yesterday and she never says anything about the accident and I don't like to press her – oh dear, press her!

MAC. You were speaking to her? But I thought you said she was...

WILSON. Dead, dear? Oh, she is – as a doorbell.

MAC. Then how...

WILSON. They're always coming through to me, Mary dear – the spirits. They contact me in all sorts of ways.

MAC. Really?

WILSON. I've seen that septical look before – you think I'm a bit of a fruit pie – one sandwich short of a lunch box.

MAC. No. Not at all.

WILSON. Don't worry, dear. I'm used to it. But they do talk to me, you know. Mostly in my head but quite often they'll come through the electrical appliances – the radio or the phone, even the blender on occasion.

MAC. The blender?

WILSON. Yes. Sometimes the messages are quite difficult to work out, too. When Avril first came through it was just a lot of nonsense about armchairs and sofas and fridges – till I made the furniture van connection and knew it was her.

MAC. Oh, yes, the van that knocked her…

WILSON. I think she would approve of you.

MAC. I hope you won't be offended but I'm not really in the market for a new…er…relationship.

WILSON. Just dinner, honestly, no pressure.

MAC. Good. Because to tell you the truth, I'm a bit off men at the moment.

WILSON. I'm not surprised, dear. I heard about your fiancé dumping you.

MAC. Well, I wouldn't put it quite like…

WILSON. That's why I thought why not ask that nice Mary at Terry's work round for dinner – she must be feeling a bit low after her fiancé ran off with the cleaner.

MAC. She wasn't…she ran her own industrial cleaning agency and…

WILSON. Better to find out now that he was unsuitable – you don't want to marry a man who goes weak at the legs at the sight of a bri-nylon overall.

MAC. She didn't wear… Mrs Wilson…

WILSON. Mary.

MAC. I'm really surprised that Terry would want me here – frankly we're not all that close at work.

WILSON. Nonsense – it will be a nice surprise for him.

MAC. You mean he doesn't know I'm coming?

WILSON. He'd only vertigo the idea. He doesn't like to socialise with people from work. He says they're all boring.

MAC. I see.

WILSON. Oh not you, dear. He hardly knows you. No it's probably because when you teachers get together you talk shopping. Goodness, where is that boy? My chicken will have dried out completely. He can't pass that pub and come straight home.

MAC. Terry lives with you?

WILSON. He moved back after…he was just rolling around in that big house of his and Avril's – I said when they bought it I don't know why you want to go buying something that size; it'll just be a seagull round your neck. Anyway, it's up for sale. Avril agrees he should look for something smaller once it's sold. What about you, dear?

MAC. I moved back with my mother after Brian and I…we had a flat.

WILSON. I always say you should never share a bathroom until after you're married. Still, nothing like going back to Mum, eh?

MAC. Well, my mother's getting on a bit and she gets a bit…confused sometimes, but…

WILSON. I must check my chicken – don't want us getting E Colon. You sure you don't want a drink just now?

MAC. Well, actually…

WILSON. Fine. I'll be back DOA.

(She exits to the kitchen.)

MAC. God, what a nightmare. *(She dials a number on her mobile phone.)* Hello, Mum, it's me. Mary. Your daughter. Now, listen, I want you to phone me on my mobile in five minutes. No you phone me. Yes I know I phoned you but I want you to call me back on my mobile. What do you mean you can't find it? I have it here. I'm phoning you from it. Use *your* phone to call *my* mobile. Say that it's an emergency and you want me home straight away. No there's no emergency, I just want you to say there is. I'm at a friend from work's – Terry Wilson – yes Briar Road, how did you…you know his mother? Mum, you two didn't— never mind. Just call me about the emergency and get me out of here. *Make up* an emergency. I don't know – anything – say the cat's on fire or something. Mum. Mum. Are you still there? *(pause)* Where were you? Listen. Listen! Just phone – I'll do the rest. What? Brian? What does he want? No, Mother, I don't want to speak to him after what he did to me. No don't let him in – look, I'll be home soon. Call me in five minutes. *(She rings off.)* I must get another appointment with Dr Grant.

(She puts the phone down, eyeing it anxiously. **WILSON** *enters.)*

WILSON. Still a pit pink. I don't understand it – it's been in for ages. You're looking a little bit pale, dear. Anything wrong?

MAC. Well…

WILSON. Tell you what, why don't you go and freshen up before Terry gets here? Put on some lipstick – there's nothing makes you feel rejuveniled like a bit of, what is it you youngsters call it, slapper?

MAC. Slap. Yes. Perhaps I will just…

WILSON. I'll show you where the bathroom is – use the upstairs one – it's got a better mirror. And I'll just check the veg.

(They exit. After a moment, **TERRY** *and* **MARY LEVIN** *enter. The latter is clearly inebriated.)*

TERRY. No, Mary, I'm sure Mum won't mind.

LEVIN. Oopsadaisy. I knew I shouldn't have had those last three pintsh. I really should get home.

TERRY. I think you need cheering up – a bit of company. You looked so miserable sitting at that bar.

LEVIN. If you're sure your mother will be OK about it.

TERRY. No. She is always nagging me to bring women back – friends round. Better than propping that bar up all night. That's if you can survive Mum's cooking. Just pray it isn't chicken.

LEVIN. Lisshen, I don't make a habit of propping up a bra as you call it. *(giggles)* A bar, I mean. *(giggles)* Propping up a bra, oh dear.

TERRY. I expect you have no choice about the bra. *(He begins to illustrate his point in dumb show, before thinking better of it.)* Ha, ha. Yeees. No, I understand. When Avril passed on, I hit the pub pretty hard. Drown my sorrows. I expect your boyfriend leaving like that... He must have been pretty special.

LEVIN. He was a bashtard.

TERRY. Right. Drink?

LEVIN. Why not? G and T.

TERRY. We appear to be out of tonic.

LEVIN. Just G then. *(giggles)*

TERRY. Generally, I don't speak to strange women in bars. Oh I don't mean you're strange, Mary. It's just that I haven't socialised much since my wife... *(He trails off.)*

LEVIN. Died. Since your wife died. You have to say it Barry.

TERRY. Terry, yes.

LEVIN. I like to call a spade a spade. I mean what's all that passed on stuff. When I need to pee I don't ask where the bathroom is or ask to wash my hands.

TERRY. Isn't that a bit unhygienic? Ha, ha.

LEVIN. You're a funny man, Barry.

TERRY. Terry, yes. Here's your er G.

LEVIN. Bottoms up. *(She swallows it down in one gulp.)* While you're still on your feet, put another one in there.

TERRY. Oh, er right. Don't you think... Right.

LEVIN. I didn't build up my own business by being hypocratical and sycophitic; hyposicical and sypocrantic; hyp...a creepy crawler. They told me the world of industrial cleaning was a man's world. So I had to be strong; tougher than the competition; stronger than the men. *(She bursts into tears.)* Waah!

TERRY. Oh, don't, er…

LEVIN. Sorry. Sorry. I never do this. It's just. Waah!

TERRY. I understand. Your relationship has just ended. It's a loss like any other. When I lost Avril…

LEVIN. You didn't lose her, Barry. You didn't misplace her in the aisles at Tesco's. She DIED. I didn't LOSE my boyfriend – he left me because he decided he still loved his fiancée. But I'm strong enough to say it out loud, strong enough to face the fact that he's left me. Waah!

TERRY. Please, Mary, try to get a hold of yourself. Here, have a sip of your drink.

(She downs it in one.)

LEVIN. Get me another one.

TERRY. Don't you think you ought to slow down?

LEVIN. No. I'm going to live a life in the fasht lane. Lisshen, I hope you didn't get me here thinking I'd be eashy to shedush. Secudsh. Bed.

TERRY. No, not at all. I've hardly thought about…that… since Avril… As I said, I thought you looked a bit miserable and lonely and…

LEVIN. Becaush I have to warn you I am not some common tart. I am…shopishtic…shophishtic…shophish…posh.

TERRY. Of coursh… I mean, of course.

LEVIN. I run my own bishnesh you know. I can wear posh frocks. I have posh friends and I can talk posh. I am a posh lady. Hell. Where's the bog? I need to puke.

TERRY. Use the downstairs one – first on the left.

*(**LEVIN** exits. **MAC**'s mobile rings.)*

TERRY. Hello. Yes, Mary's here. She's not available at the moment. She's…er…just being sick. Can I get her to call you…an emergency you say? Sorry, can you repeat that – I thought you said the cat was on fire. Ha, ha. No, no, she's just had a bit too much to drink, that's all. What? Teetotal? You could have fooled me. She's certainly fallen off the wagon tonight. No – the wagon. No, she hasn't had an accident. Look who shall I say… someone at the door?… Yes, I'll hold. *(Pause. He goes to the door and calls off.)* Mary, are you all right? There's someone on the… What? I'm just coming. Damn – she'll call back if it's urgent.

(He rings off, puts the phone down and exits. **WILSON** *enters.)*

WILSON. Terry? Where have you got to?

*(***MAC***'s phone rings.)*

Terry. Phone. *(She answers the phone.)* Hello. Yes, this is Mary speaking. Mother? Mother, I haven't heard from you since you came through the cooker. How are you and Dad? I know he's dead, dear, you both are. How are things on the other side? Do you have any messages to pass on? You're confused? What man? The cat? Mother, slow down. Is there anyone there with you? Brian? And whom does Brian wish to contact? Me? No, you must open the door to him – we must hear what he has to say. Mother? Where's she gone?

(She rings off as **TERRY** *enters.)*

Ah, I thought I heard you coming in dear. Where on earth have you been till this time?

TERRY. I went to the pub. Who was on the phone?

WILSON. Mother.

TERRY. God, not again. It's embarrassing enough when you talk to them on the blender.

WILSON. She gave me the most peculiar message – something about burning cats and a Brian at the door. Anyway…

WILSON & TERRY. *(together)* Listen, I hope you don't mind but…what?

WILSON. I was going to say, you know how I met that nice Mary?

TERRY. You met her? Was that when she was rushing for the loo?

WILSON. Yes, she's in the bathroom. Nothing like a bit of old slapper to brighten you up.

TERRY. Mum, she's not a slapper. It's just she's had a bit of boyfriend trouble recently.

WILSON. Fiancé.

TERRY. No, I don't think it had gone that far. She's had a bit too much to drink and...

WILSON. Really – she told me she didn't. Anyway, she's looking forward to her chicken.

TERRY. That should settle her stomach.

WILSON. You will have your little joke. Come and help me carve it, dear. And you can cut the nice tart I've baked for pudding into slices.

TERRY. I'll just get my chisel out of the toolbox.

(They exit. MAC enters and dials her mobile.)

MAC. Mother, why haven't you phoned? No, Mother, of course I'm not sick. Fallen off the wagon? What? Brian? Why did you let him in? No, I didn't. No, Mother , I don't want to... Brian, we've talked enough. It's too late for that. I did love you till that cow came along and... I don't want to see you. Don't say that, I'm too upset to... you were such a bastard. No! No! Put my mother on. No, don't call me later. Mother? Get rid of him. Well put him back out again. Phone me when he's gone. *(She rings off, tearfully.)* Damn. I just put this mascara on.

(She exits. LEVIN enters.)

LEVIN. Yoo hoo. I'm feeling a bet bitter, a bit bitter, a bit better. I think I got some suck on your rig. Perhapsh I'll have another, just to settle my stomach. *(She pours herself a gin. Before she can drink it the phone rings and she answers it.)* Yesh. Mary speaking. Mum? Yesh you sound funny, too. I'm a little bit intosh…intoxich…intocsh… Pissed. What? Brian's hanging around outside? Get him in. No. Get him in. *(pause)* Brian. Darling, of course I'll see you. No it musht be this line. Yesh I want you back my darling – I haven't changed my mind. It might seem like two minutes ago I called you a bashtard but that was because I thought you were going back to her. Wait at Mum's for me – I'll be right round. He wants me back. Yipee! *(She downs the gin.)* Ooh, I feel a bit…

(Still clutching the phone, she collapses behind the sofa, concealing her from others entering the room.)

(WILSON and **TERRY** *enter.)*

TERRY. I still think that chicken looks a bit raw in the middle.

WILSON. Nonsense, dear, I used one of those gormless cook recipes.

TERRY. I'm sure.

WILSON. And there's a nice patio for starters.

TERRY. I'll give the dentist a precautionary call.

WILSON. I'm sure Mary will like it. I'm so glad you're all right about this, son. I know you think Avril's hardly cold in the ground.

TERRY. She isn't in the ground. I scattered her ashes in the Botanical Gardens where we met, remember?

WILSON. Yes, a lovely romantic gesture – reminding you of your first meeting. Just like me and your father. Though there was a bit of a fuss when I scattered his ashes – we met in the swimming pool at the public baths.

TERRY. Anyway, it's OK. It's about time I had some female company again and at least it's not one of your misguided attempts at match-making.

*(***MAC** *enters.)*

WILSON. Ah, there you are, dear. I thought you'd fallen down the pan. Oh, you do look nice. Don't you think she looks nice, Terry?

TERRY. What? When?

WILSON. Don't just stand there looking like a bat out of water, Terry. Sit down. *(looking uneasily towards the door, he sits on the sofa)* You, too, Mary. No not on that chair – sit next to Terry.

MAC. Well, I…

TERRY. Mum!

WILSON. It's just that chair is always embarrassing guests. It always makes a farting noise every time anyone moves around in it – and, of course, people move around in it all the time just to show that it was the chair. Before you can blink it sounds like the aftermath of a baked bean eating competition in here.

TERRY. Mum!

WILSON. Forgive me, dear, for being so unsensitive.

TERRY. Thank you.

WILSON. Banging on about the furniture.

TERRY. Furniture?

WILSON. You know – furniture van – Avril.

TERRY. That hadn't even crossed my mind.

MAC. Till now.

WILSON. Well, isn't this nice?

TERRY. Mum, there's something you should know. When you said you'd met Mary…

WILSON. So it's gym you teach then, is it, Mary?

MAC. Modern languages.

WILSON. Oh, I thought it was gym – it ought to be with your figure. Hasn't she got a nice figure, Terry?

TERRY. Yes, very nice, but…

WILSON. You look as if you, what is it you youngsters call it, pump steel? Terry used to play a lot of badminton with Avril – she does miss it on the other side. Do you play, Mary?

MAC. No.

WILSON. Pity, you could have given Terry a game. Now what about a nice whisky, Mary?

MAC. As I told you, I never touch alcohol.

WILSON. You don't have to pretend to me, dear. Terry's told me about you swilling back the booze.

MAC. What?

TERRY. No, I…

WILSON. Have some dips then pass them around, Terry. No, not that one – it's garlic – you might get a shag later.

TERRY. What?

MAC. A snog. She means you might get a…snog.

(horribly embarrassed pause)

WILSON. Terry, you're sitting there on grappling hooks. Why do you keep looking over there? Pay some attention to your guest. I think you'll discover she's not as boring as you might have thought.

MAC. Thanks.

TERRY. Mum, speaking of guests…

WILSON. I'm sure you two would like a nice chat without me being a raspberry so I'll just sort out the starters – guess what we're having?

MAC. Shit!

TERRY. You're getting warm.

MAC. Sorry, but I seem to have lost my mobile.

WILSON. Where did you have it last, dear, above your bed?

MAC. My mobile phone. I had it here.

TERRY. I'll just have a quick scout around the house – see if I can find it.

(He exits hurriedly.)

WILSON. Perhaps you left it in the toilet.

MAC. I don't think… I'll just check.

(She exits.)

WILSON. It's like Paddington Circus in here.

*(**LEVIN**'s voice is heard from behind the sofa.)*

LEVIN. Where am I?

WILSON. Ooh the voices. Who is this? Speak. You're through to Mary, dear. What is your message?

LEVIN. I can't seem to get up.

WILSON. Go towards the light. Who are you?

LEVIN. Mary.

WILSON. Yes?

LEVIN. It's Mary.

WILSON. That's right, dear.

LEVIN. I feel as if I've been through the blender.

WILSON. Oh, we've spoken before then?

LEVIN. Is Barry there?

WILSON. Yes, you have a message for Barry?

*(**TERRY** and **MAC** enter.)*

TERRY. Mum, has anyone been here?

WILSON. There's someone here now, trying to make contact – a lost soul.

TERRY. Speaking of lost – I seem to have lost, well mislaid… Aah!

*(**LEVIN** suddenly springs up from behind the sofa. Everyone reacts in fright. **MAC** falls back in shock into the chair she has been told to avoid, generating the farting sound she had been cautioned about, immediately causing her to spring up again.)*

LEVIN. Phew! I think I must have had a little accident.

TERRY. I think we all have.

LEVIN. Wooh! I feel ready for anything after that little lie down. *(She begins to wobble.)*

TERRY. Best sit down. Er... Mother, this is Mary; Mary this is my mother, Mary... er, Mrs Wilson, and Mary this is er, Mary.

MAC. That's my mobile.

LEVIN. Oh. *(Dazedly she hands it over.)*

WILSON. Why was she hiding behind the sofa?

TERRY. She must have...

WILSON. Pretending to be one of my spirits.

LEVIN. No more spirits for me, thanksh. I could probably manage a lager.

TERRY. Perhaps you've had enough.

LEVIN. Just to celebrate.

(Mobile rings. MAC answers it.)

MAC. Mother, what on earth is... What? I told you to get rid of him. Well, tell him to leave. What do you mean he's going in and out like a fiddler's elbow? Brian? I thought I'd made things perfectly clear. I am not schizophrenic. No you can't come round here. Brian? *(She rings off.)* I think you'll have to excuse me.

LEVIN. My boyfriend wants me back.

TERRY. When did you find this out?

WILSON. You stay here, dear, I'll sort this out. Terry, is this young la— woman a friend of yours?

TERRY. I was trying to tell you – we met tonight. I asked her back here for a bite to eat. Her boyfriend had just left her. She seemed really sad.

*(**LEVIN** meanwhile has begun to sing a drunken version of a romantic song, garbling the lyrics. The original production used Mary Wells' "My Guy," with lyrics like "I'm sticking to my guy like a bird to a letter," but there is room for invention here.)*

WILSON. Well, she seems happy enough now, dear.

MAC. Listen, that was my mother – a bit of an emergency – the cat – she's had to call in the vet.

WILSON. Just stay a while longer, dear – it's all right, we're not having any menagerie a troy here. Terry, you ought to see Mary home.

MAC. No, honestly, I have a car.

WILSON. You can't possibly drive in your condition. Anyway, I meant this one. She's obviously abbreviated.

LEVIN. I'm shtarved. Is there anything to eat? You said I could come for tea.

WILSON. Really, Terry, there's not enough chicken to go round.

TERRY. She's more than welcome to mine.

WILSON. Terry!

TERRY. OK. OK.

(LEVIN *finds the crisps and begins to eat them.*)

MAC. Look, there's no need – I'm just going. If someone called Brian should call here...

WILSON. That name tolls a bell.

LEVIN. Brian? My Brian?

MAC. No, my Brian. That is, he's not my Brian any more. The trouble is he may turn up here.

WILSON. I hope you'll tell him where to go after the way he's treated you.

TERRY. Mum, it's none of our business.

LEVIN. I'd grab him with both handsh if I were you.

MAC. Yes, I'm sure you would but some of us are a bit more choosy.

LEVIN. If you can afford to be.

MAC. What's that supposed to mean?

LEVIN. If you want to keep a man, you'll have to lighten up doll – unstarch your underwear.

MAC. I expect you have trouble most of the time remembering where you mislaid yours.

LEVIN. What did she just shay? Is she saying I'm promish, promicu, easy?

WILSON. I really don't think you should be discussing underwear in front of Terry. Remember he's been halibut since Avril died.

TERRY. Mum! Look why don't we all just settle down. This has obviously been a bit of a misunderstanding. Let's not spoil the evening. It's not all bad – there isn't enough chicken to go around for a start. Ha. Ha. *(pause)* What a coincidence though, eh? Mum and I both invited someone called Mary round for tea.

WILSON. And they've both been dumped by someone called Brian.

(TERRY looks worried.)

TERRY. Yeees, that is a coincidence. Naah. Naah. It couldn't be.

LEVIN. Where's my lager?

MAC. I really do have to go.

WILSON. Well, if you must. Perhaps we can arrange to have you round later in the week. How are you for Sunday? I do a lovely joint on Sundays.

TERRY. We smoke that and we don't notice the food. Ha. Ha. Just kidding, Mum. I should talk – I'm pretty useless when it comes to cooking.

MAC. Well, must fly.

TERRY. Yes, of course. I hope the cat's all right.

MAC. What cat? Oh, the cat. Yes.

(TERRY and MAC exit.)

WILSON. Perhaps it's time you were getting home too, dear.

LEVIN. God, you're right! Brian's round at my mother's. I have to go there. *(She stands.)* Ooh, dizzy. I think I have to go to the toilet again. *(She knocks over the crisps.)* Shorry. Shorry. I'll clean them up when I get a back. I'm an exshpert in cleaning. I run my own business, you know.

(She exits.)

WILSON. That's nice, dear. *(pause, while the penny drops)* Cleaning business? Oh, my word.

*(**TERRY** and **MAC** return.)*

TERRY. Mum, Mary's just spotted her fiancé coming up the garden path.

WILSON & MAC. *(together)* He mustn't come in!

MAC. I didn't realise you felt so strongly about it, Mrs Wilson.

*(During the next speech **WILSON** tries to signal the situation to an increasingly confused **TERRY**. The mime might include some pointing towards the toilet, some cleaning motions, appearing drunk, etc.)*

MAC. If you could just say I'm not here. I don't think it's a good idea to speak to him just now. Maybe when things have calmed down a bit. At the moment it's all so raw. I still feel if I met that woman he ran off with I'd tear her limb from limb. *(She notices **WILSON**.)* Er…

WILSON. It's that Brian that makes me sick, dear.

(Doorbell sounds.)

You go, Terry.

TERRY. Me?

WILSON & MAC. *(together)* Make sure you get rid of him.

*(**MAC** regards **WILSON** with surprise as **TERRY** exits. The sound of voices becoming increasingly heated should become apparent in the course of the scene.)*

WILSON. Sit down, dear. Have a crisp. Oh, no – that dreadful woman's spilled the lot. Still there are worse things she could have done, eh? Though crisp spilling is pretty terrible.

MAC. I can understand why she's so upset – I could easily get drunk to try to forget everything, too. But I never touch it.

WILSON. It's never too late to start.

MAC. What?

WILSON. Come on. Let's get fish faced.

(**LEVIN** *enters.*)

LEVIN. That's better. What's that noise at the front door?

WILSON. Nothing, dear. Terry's having a bit of an argument with the man who cleans the bins. He claims we didn't pay last week.

LEVIN. Let me deal with it. I deal with cleaners every day.

MAC. How's that then?

WILSON. Her house is absolutely filthy.

LEVIN. Pardon?

MAC. She might as well know – my fiancé's at the door, insisting on seeing me. I don't know how he thinks I can ever forgive him for running off with a cheap little slut.

WILSON. I'm sure she's probably a very nice girl – a hexagon of virtue.

LEVIN. Forgive and forget, doll. I'm taking my boyfriend back. He's seen what a mistake it was to go back to that frozen virgin he was engaged to.

MAC. There's nothing wrong with being a virgin.

WILSON. Of course there isn't. I was one forty years ago.

LEVIN. She could say no in four languages.

MAC. What did you say you did again?

WILSON. She's in executioner management.

*(The next exchange should be like internal monologues till both **LEVIN** and **MAC** become aware of the similarities.)*

LEVIN. She kept trying to change him.

MAC. He needed to change.

LEVIN. I mean he had this cute old cord jacket.

MAC. He had a manky old cord jacket.

LEVIN. And a nice little thin moustache.

MAC. And this absurd little moustache.

LEVIN. Made him look like an old fashioned movie star.

MAC. Made him look like a spiv.

BOTH. Now he's clean shaven and wears a suit, he looks like a bank manager.

(They stop and regard each other.)

WILSON. Ooh, they could be identikit twins.

*(***TERRY** *enters.)*

TERRY. He refuses to go till he's spoken to... *(He notices the atmosphere.)* Mary.

WILSON. The girls were just telling me about their similar taste in men, dear.

BOTH WOMEN. You!

MAC. You're the slut who ran off with Brian.

TERRY. Of course she isn't.

WILSON. I'm afraid she is the slut, dear.

LEVIN. You're the frigid virgin.

TERRY. Of course she isn't.

WILSON. Yes, she's the frigid virgin all right, dear.

BOTH WOMEN. I could kill you!

TERRY. Of course you couldn't.

WILSON. I think they probably could, dear.

LEVIN. Witch!

MAC. Tart!

WILSON. What a good idea – let's all have a nice piece of tart. Terry, come with me to help. And get the first aid kit.

TERRY. What about Brian?

(He is ushered off by **WILSON.***)*

LEVIN. He's come to get me.

MAC. You're more stupid than you look – he's come to see me.

LEVIN. I'm going to him.

MAC. Go. You're welcome to him.

*(***LEVIN** *exits.* **MAC** *fumes, then, on impulse, pours herself a drink.)*

MAC. Right, I will get fish-faced.

(She swallows it back and starts coughing and gagging. **LEVIN** *returns.)*

LEVIN. He saw me, looked shocked and took off down the path.

MAC. Told you, didn't I?

LEVIN. He always said you were a smug cow. *(She punches* **MAC** *who falls behind the sofa.* **LEVIN** *rushes off.)* Brian, wait for me – she definitely doesn't want you any more.

*(***TERRY** *and* **WILSON** *tentatively return.)*

TERRY. The coast's clear. They've gone.

WILSON. Thank heavens – I was worried they'd both be lying on the floor – I thought you were going to have to give them artificial insemination. Son – this is all my fault for interfering. It's just I didn't want you to end up like me – when your father was gone, I had a lot of lonely years.

TERRY. I know, Mum. You meant well. Who'd have thought it, eh? Hey, the chicken will be cold now; what say I go for a take away?

WILSON. Nonsense, dear, we can eat it cold, on sandwiches.

TERRY. Oh. All right. If you insist. I'll do it – just you sit there – you've had enough excitement for one evening.

WILSON. You can say that again – I thought there was going to be a blood bank.

TERRY. You mean…never mind. Thanks, mum.

WILSON. What for, dear?

TERRY. Just thanks.

(He exits.)

WILSON. Peace at last. It's been condominium in here.

*(***MAC** *begins to groan from behind the sofa.)*

MAC. Oooh! My head.

WILSON. Oh dear, the spirits. Hello! You're through to Mary, dear. What is your message?

MAC. I've been knocked down.

WILSON. Avril, is that you?

(Blackout.)

Lightning Source UK Ltd.
Milton Keynes UK
UKOW03f1000050114

224003UK00001B/4/P